Verba Sequentur

"Rem tene verba sequentur"

Know your stuff and the words will follow

Cato the Censor
(234 - 149 BCE)

Published in 2021 by Birdfish Books
www.birdfishbooks.com.au

All rights reserved. No part of this edition
of this text may be reproduced or transmitted
in any form or by any means, electronic
or mechanical, including photocopy, recording
or any informational storage and retrieval system,
without prior permission from the publisher.

Cover image: 'John Flaus' by Dave Purdon of Taradale

ISBN-13: 978-0-9953718-7-3

BIRDFISH BOOKS

Verba Sequentur

by John Flaus

Acknowledgements

'Where Did I Put Those Knitting Patterns?' was previously published in *Shots from the Chamber*: Pomonal Publishing, 2016
'Amok Summery of Bloomsday' was previously published in *Selected Irish Writers from His Library*: Locust Hill Press, 2001.
'A Country Road, A Tree'; 'For the Record' and 'One Fantasy after Another' previously published in *Parallacts*, by John Flaus: Mark Time Books, 2012

Contents

First Cause	7
Advahnce Australia Fair	8
Keep Your Eyes on the Road	9
Making Butter	10
Making Honey	11
Old Dawn	12
New Dawn	13
Where Did I Put Those Knitting Patterns?	14
Us	15
To The Woman in White	16
Emily Dickinson Regards Her Portrait	17
Laurels	18
Dualities	20
Experience	21
East of Eternity	22
Captivated and Confounded	23
The Scheme of Things	24
Body Count	26
The Umbrellas Of Cherbourg	28
S–21 The House of Pain	29
The Confidential Dark	30
Moonbright Man of the Sky	32
Ern Melee *or* A Hoax of a Diffident Choler	33
The Best Boss I Ever Had	34
To the Daughter of a Friend	36
Remembering Darcy Waters	37
Parallacts	38
Amok Summery of Bloomsday	40
Notes	49

First Cause

First there was darkness darker than night
Whence matter, bidden, came to be,
By that creator, the uncreated He
Who was All, but all alone before the light;
All powerful yet powerless One,
For want of subject — master's differend,
For want of meaning — subject's end,
Some Other, that discourse might be done.

One and not-One, He bound to he as he to she,
Thus the first causation: His command
Prefiguring man — that discursive he
Who rashly maketh reason prove absurd;
Almighty He wrought chaos 'neath His hand
To bring forth order, purpose and the Word.

Advahnce Australia Fair

Come on down, come by, come buy,
Now's the time to spend tomorrow's pay
For every day's a trading day.
Fill the coffers where our fortunes lie,
Help feed the furnace of economy!
There was virtue once in saving,
Now consumption is our craving;
Help raise the index of prosperity!

No need to ponder deep on market forces —
Borrow! For the bounty of the earth will never end.
Bargain with our sunburnt country's rare resources.
Come along, citizens, do your duty,
Bravely spend, for we will lend.
Let your debts become our booty.

Keep Your Eyes on the Road
For the ghosts

Mile after mile the road unribbons,
Passing paddocks stark and shaven,
Nothing much to see: scattered land-wrack,
Native tussocks giving ground to hardy thistles.
That's why we leave the stubborn bastards standing,
They're our scrawny testament of occupation.
We worked the land and ploughed a nation in
While unnamed species scurried to extinction.
Two centuries it took, or thereabouts,
Time enough to arrogate a continent.

Careful, there's a crossing coming up —
Signs, nothing special, just words and such:
Keep Out — that's the one you see the most
(Except in Tasmania, where it's *Strawberries*).
Private Property — now there's a word to ponder,
Not *Property*, that's plain enough,
But *Private* — hah, there's values there!
The common good and sacred rights of citizens,
We the people hereby declare our dependence
On distant deals and prices in contention.

Trespassers — some kind of sinners, aren't they?
Like invaders, unlicensed users of the land?
Well, invasion's something we won't stand for,
Not here, not in this proud country.
Keep Out, Keep Out — so who's that meant for?

Making Butter

With toil and patience fill the crocks,
Wind and wind the wheeling grind,
Will and skill store nature's stocks.

Hard are the ways which hi-tech mocks
(These user-friendly days, to ease inclined),
With toil and patience fill the crocks.

Nature's rhythms make no use of clocks,
"Productivity" devalues hand and mind,
Will and skill store nature's stocks.

Tiring turn on turn, till jarring blocks,
Old routine between machine and muscle find,
With toil and patience fill the crocks.

And when the churn on third turn locks —
Push on; soul and sinew work aligned.
Will and skill store nature's stocks.

Push, against circleward sinews' shocks,
Wind and wind the wheeling grind,
With toil and patience fill the crocks.
Will and skill store nature's stocks.

Making Honey

Good workers' famed epitome,
Builders of the comb, dwellers of the hive,
Might yet their beedom glory be!

The flowing nectar's far flung military
Do day long strive that all may thrive.
Good workers' famed epitome.

True wealth they gain from life's economy,
Which needs not another's worth deprive.
Might yet their beedom glory be!

True gold they gain from life's metallurgy,
Treasure such as glitters not, but glowing and alive.
Good workers' famed epitome

Warmly hued and coolly molten mystery
Whereof we our sweeted feasts derive.
Might yet their beedom glory be!

Dedication, enterprise and industry,
We seek in similes such values to revive,
Good workers' famed epitome.
Might not their beedom boredom be?

Old Dawn

O bard be mindful, song and subject intersect
Only in the easeful retrospect of danger past.
Whispers in the dark when loins and coiling limbs hold fast
Are woven as the words of love long after made perfect.
Heaven's gate we picklocked in the watches of the night,
There entered we in practised furtive haste
And from Eve's tree forbidden flesh did taste,
Until the lark's ascending song made call to flight.

O bard unbind me, sing against such sanctions cruel,
To soothe that ulcer, guilt, like vain Laocoons we strove,
That thrall whereby grey men adjure us all to jealous rule.
Our nightly paradise renew, a radiant myth construct,
For more than passing joy we knew when in this budding grove
'Midst silver beams 'neath golden boughs we fucked.

New Dawn

O bard be mindful, gold enamelling may well reflect
Only in the easeful retrospect of sated chase.
Whispers in the dark when loins and coiling limbs embrace
Are woven in the words of love long after made subject
To rhyme and rhythm. Poesy's by subtler passion driven
Than the storms of little deaths we've nightly entertained,
Short eternities so sweetly spent and rapturously regained,
Raptures full and flooding, taken fiercely, gently given.

O bard unbind me, for I have other promises to keep,
A fence to mend and swales to dig before next darkness falls.
If it be within your bardic power, yet in this hour bid it sleep,
Do not entreat the sun stand still before first dawning's hue.
'Pies are gargling in the paddocks, milkers tramping in the stalls,
And the mortgaged duties of the day more needful
                              than my mad need for you.

Where Did I Put Those Knitting Patterns?

I found his glasses today — or, rather,
They found me. It was just a present chore
To put the past behind a little further —
Like love's rapture, mourning's term is brief.
They nestled out of sight, for eyes no more,
As still as a spider, outwaiting grief.

The ache is ebbed, the loss less keen,
Stitched up in years we think content.
It embraces us, our dear routine,
Wipes daily surface clean, disperses dust,
Each day makes do, all passion spent,
While settled hearts in solace rust.

Until — the stab of memory, its sting,
Unlike long yesterday, unplanned.
Webbed in time, inert, some Thing
We didn't think to find
Untimely comes to hand
And thus to mind.

Us

Oddly assorted
Yet strangely compatible,
Lately we courted,
A couple for life.

To The Woman in White

Thou still unravished bride of Amherst,
Swathed in scholars' speculations,
Keep thy secrets.

No fury more sedate than thine;
None more shrewdly yet remark
The commonplace divine,

Wherein thy cryptic joy
Stood brow to brow with Beauty,
Made obeisance erect to Awe.

Nor may Logic sound thy lucid mystery —
Such paraphrase can scarce be writ:
As fewer — More!

Is there room within that carriage
Whose steeds turn towards Eternity?
Charmed singer on the charnel steps,
Turn and see, wait for me.

Emily Dickinson Regards Her Portrait

When now I look,
That whom I see
— a Face — makes claim
My name from me.

If line and limn
Make less of me,
Take life and limb,
And leave — Infinity!

Laurels

At the sirens' call, a caution:
Be not bid.
They'll have your mind for auction,
Soon be rid.

Jabber not with goblin jobbers,
Pay heed none.
Be not smeared with adulation,
Next day gone.

They know not you nor wish to,
Mark them well.
Mountebanks in borrowed brightness
Buy and sell.

Renown perceives itself, not thee,
Pluck it out.
Ever faint of faith and fickle
Put to rout.

Celebrity's a glister, soon turns sour,
Time's the proof.
From proud triumph's proffered revelry
Stand aloof.

The gilded champions leave no footprint
After glory's got.
With garlands, sack and silver
Ply me not.

Fame is but the bauble,
I'm the whore.
Prise the user's pennies,
Nothing more.

Dualities

In weary work and play
The body burns the day.
Quickened by the night
The quiet soul shines bright.

In the body's business
The soul may sometime rest.
In the body's rapture
The soul is put to test.

Experience

If skin were wax
Its glaze no care could roughen,
Its glow by custom firmed
Could ardour rarely soften.

If soul were wax
It might with passion melt,
Its form by reason cooled
Re-drawn as fitly felt.

East of Eternity

With darkness waits the day,
In diurnal duty bound;
Only if it die
Can forever come around.

Captivated and Confounded

Reaching out to Spenser,
Looking hard at Gray,
Captivated by Christina,
Confounded, but, by Emily.

The Scheme of Things
After 'The Locket'

Two armies came, advancing on the plain,
And raised a roar with rebel yell and cannon.
Smaller creatures and their hunters fled or perished,
Ravens, scattered from their roosts,
Flew to refuge in the ringing crags.

It's the nature of things — or so they say —
That men must fight and nations go to war.
What nature's this? What creatures kill their kind?
Upright Yankee and Ohio farm boy in the name of Union,
Courteous creole, landless cajun, before their time
Believers in the dream beyond the teeming shore.

What brought them here to hell on earth —
A call to arms, a cause — what else?
Musty virtues spun from Book and trade,
Occluded conscience, tattered gallantry,
Adventure — the blithe resort of wasters,
Or worse, that beckoning whore called History?

They dispute in fear and rage the furious morning.
Now the battle's won, the war moves on,
And Death is left to count its trophies:
Banners, tunics, bodies, torn and bloodied.
It's the making of a nation — or so they say.

Still perch the watchers 'til disturbance dies.
With unblinking corvine gravity they wait
While groans give way to silence
With the saddened sunlit passing of the day;
Then, true to nature, take slow wing
And circle downward to the plain.

Body Count
After 'Merrill's Marauders'

— Walawbum, Burma 1944 —

Did Lemchek make it? I saw him get hit!
The silver tongues spoke and we answered the call,
The spirit was with us, we were fit for killing.
Emboldened in our new bred bastardry
We sailed a sea and trudged a timeless jungle,
Found life's meaning in the slime of war.

So the world comes down to this:
Percussion, smoke and splinters —
Close field of vision, short arc of fire.
Luck and hot death go head to head,
And all the swelter and the slogging's worth it
When the red lust rises
And the bayonet's thirsty work gets done.
Butchers all, we band of brothers.

Did Lemchek make it? Did Lemchek make it?
After battle, battered and wrung,
Life creeps in around the edges,
Bathed in blood and drool, pus and tears,
— the natural secretions of victory.
Now the brigadier must make his ministrations,
Muttered comforts for the damaged and the dying;
Not for them at journey's end a two-faced medal
And the nation's praise embalmed in brazen psalms.

Did Lemchek make it? I saw him get hit!
Stretchered under plasma, yet he rises in galvanic frenzy,
With skinny hand and unseeing eye he clutches at his leader.
In life's last strangled breath, still he pleads to know:
Did — Lemchek — make — it?
The crazy claw unclutches, falls,
The medic's steady hand unhooks the line.
They lay him down in glory, mucked and stinking,
As cold as the lies of smiling men.

"Did Lemchek make it?"… "He's Lemchek."

The Umbrellas of Cherbourg
After 'Les Parapluies de Cherbourg'

Beneath umbrellas slicked and streaming
See, fair Cherbourg lies,
Where music's garlands wove
Foretaste of paradise.

Those are tears upon us teeming —
When unheard melodies arise
If not our pledges prove
The song within us dies.

Unseen bonds restrain us; our screaming
Inward dumbly cries.
Where coward comforts best behove
Mute sorrows harmonise.

Only dross can come from dreaming.
Pleasures chanced in enterprise
Which once in custom's tether strove,
Submission's balms chastise.

Beneath umbrellas dark and gleaming
See, bright Cherbourg lies,
And we must dare to love
Before we can be wise.

S-21 The House of Pain

For Jim Ewing, who saw The Face

Modest whitewashed, multistoreyed school for girls,
Chastely fenced off from Phnom Pen passing by;
Once the cradle of colonial virtues,
How simply transformed to the House of Pain;
S-Dash-Twenty One: countless were those
Who writhed in torment here before
Anonymous interment in the Killing Fields.
Photographs remain, abundant "evidence",
Each in their individual agony, all in their last hour;
A speechless record, entrusted to emulsion,
Subject to time but in blind defiance of oblivion.
See this woman here — marked by torturers' dishonouring.
Yet still unbent, her gaze unyielding.

I see the one, I hear the millions:
We are the lowly dust of empires,
Strewn throughout their massing and their fall,
Roundly numbered, written off,
Collateral in the counting house of history.
No bugles sound our memory, nor cenotaphs proclaim.
O, you mighty of the earth, death's harvesters,
And you whited sepulchres, their counsellors,
Should Christ's curse be rendered true,
The depths of the sea await your descending.
You who daily fail your duties to the living,
Pay at last to us this least respect:
Find my grave. Give me a name.

The Confidential Dark

Above the hard lights and the shadows
The night bird makes its way.

That little feller used to have a dancin' spirit,
Now he waltzes, key in hand, past rows of cars
And scores their shiny sides — but feels no better for it.
That blue-rinsed gambler grips and pulls…
Maybe this time — presents for the grandkids…
No, there it goes — down the pokies' gleaming gorge.
That good wife has learned it's worse to scold
When he comes home pissed and cranky;
So she turns the other cheek, and cops another biff.

The shrouded city hums with power
And the night bird flies.

The honoured men in suits shake hands
At the meeting they never had;
The minister responsible puts down the phone
On the call she never took;
The trusted bureaucrat selects "delete"
For the document he never saw.

The night bird sees but does not know,
The city knows but does not tell.

The groaning celibate spills his seed, alone and self-forgiving,
The willing whore presents her haunches to the client,
As must the gritting bitch for his fellows in the nick,
And the flinching child at the guardian's caress.

The soft dark keeps its secrets
And the night bird flies.

Moonbright Man of the Sky

Another sacred fire has gone out.
Shelton Lea, our jovial own, our Shelley,
Rascal, scrapper, minstrel, poet,
Who knew the hard ways of the world,
Looked upon our faults and follies,
Lightly judging, darkly jesting;
Our molten miseries touched with grace.

Moonbright man of the sky,
You hunted life — grabbed it by the throat
— then with wizard words caressed it.
You took from some, gave mightily to others.
Jaunty jester running from the jacks,
Pausing, panting — time for one more puff and jug,
On your way to windswept glory!

Now your ashes with the earth are mingled.
Go, rejoin the wheel of life,
That your spirit, stark and kindly,
In such shapes as dreams be wrought,
May rise to bring us blessing.

Ern Melee *or* A Hoax of a Diffident Choler

Within the drowsing barrack walls two warrior poets lay
Fraught by mischievous invention, forestalled from martial fray.
Rancorous their rusty bugles raised in purposeful discord:
A vessel wrought of scrap unfit for ploughshare or for sword.

Malleus malevolentorum to another realm aspires
Whereof wafts fitfully the breeze that stirs the strings of liars.
Jovial as boys who sport with flies, they spun a yarn of malice,
Their ill wrought urn alembic to an oft drained chalice.

They tuned in tinkling symbols such wit they deigned to spend
To waft them on Pandora's winds whence errant muses wend.
They drank sparely of the Pierian spring; sufficed the holy spell
To hoist them with petards expressed not wisely but too well.

The Best Boss I Ever Had

For Patricia Edgar

Oppressed by circumstance, by pomp ignored,
We our daily battles wage with brave but blunted sword.
We see our dreams erode as each day make do,
And hard the inching way we haltingly pursue.

But there rise among us fiery ones,
Forged in action, fighting fit
And thirsting for the future.

I can tell of one of these
Who ascended swift the ivory tower,
Strode the corridors of power,
Seized the day and won the hour.
She shaped herself a cause to serve,
And struck a balance few can hold —
With steady nerve and tireless verve,
Sometimes cautious, sometimes bold.
Built an enclave, took command,
Enlisted thence a motley band;
She trusted some and gave free rein
But others… took in hand.

Hear this anarchist's admission:
She is the ideal autocrat if such there be,
Giving freedom in accord with task,
Not generous but genuine with praise,
Scorns flattery, and with equal force
Defends her subjects as herself.

She might have been the ideal diplomat
("Tricia, please, don't call me Pat")
If guile and patience were sufficient.
But for all her fabled toughness
In treachery she rates deficient.

She became a pioneer in the most unlikely country
Where leviathans are in contention and stakes are high —
The unfolding hearts and minds of the coming generation.

Critique alone is not enough of culture high and low,
The shrewdest diagnosis is no cure till action makes it so.
Then turned she from the groves of academe
Prepared and resolute, to realise a dream.
That dream must be negotiated,
That firm resolve must ever try
To turn the tide of Gresham's Law
(Which says that low grade drives out high).

She must palter with the corporation "suits",
So rational, soft tongued, hard eyed,
Who have paid the price of eminence —
The dream within them died.
She opens doors to talents:
Some who had their dreams put by,
Too long tethered by routine,
Now take new wings and fly.

To cast a giant shadow
We looked to models masculine,
Now in triumph as in struggle
We hail our hero feminine.

To the Daughter of a Friend

You're young — adult, yes, but young enough
To take life on the rise and smack it for a winner.
Yet none of us are victorious every time.
You strode out strongly once too often, took a fall.
Three lousy steps and half a dozen fractures,
Pulleys, splints and pins — don't want to count them all.

There you were, thinking it's your right in life
To have a good time — then twenty kinds of grief
Hit you all at once… God! Why me, this pain and strife?
And afterwards the fuss and trouble healing.
Months of rehab — that's a drag…
But through ordeal comes deeper feeling.

Yet it's not the pain so much, it's the worry:
Will it go back to normal (whatever normal was)?
Let me tell you, nothing's ever quite the same again.
'Worse' or 'better', 'nearly' — change we must endure;
'Nearly' — yes, but not ever quite as was.
That's how we grow, and — some say — mature.

Dare and crash, repent in boredom.
Ah, misery's a cruel and nagging teacher.
Well you've learned your lesson, earned your wisdom:
All of us are mincemeat in the jaws of chance
And you'll do your dough going for the long shots.
Oh unhappy truth, when all your life you've thought
— full eighteen years — that you were bullet proof.

Remembering Darcy Waters

Endure now where not enjoyment take,
Lest at life's close to nothingness we wake.
Indulgence, debts and trespasses are here attended,
Paid and paid for when poor time is ended.

Social practice seeks to formulate a person,
Liberty conditioned by law as self by role,
While care and learning by commandments rule.
We must walk strong amidst life's stumblements:
Be self, do now, make real, say true.

If hell's on earth, as oftentime it seems,
Count it lucky when it's passed in dreams.
If death leads on to life whence none return to tell,
Our dreams may be its heaven — or its hell.

When they find me cold in bed —
Make smooth my brow, unclench my hands
As livid coins look out my eyes —
Tell them I've to phantoms fled
And drunk the milk of paradise.

Parallact

Two lines, each of nine or ten syllables,
Wherein differing perspectives contend.

Life's Drama
After 'Shoulder'

The comedy of being myself,
The tragedy of not being so.

Art's Adventure
After 'What is a Poem?'

Seek not the harbour, brave the deeps —
The wave that takes you away from shore.

An Actor Prepares

What emotions do these words inspire?
But what emotions inspired these words?

One Fantasy after Another
After 'Two Lane Blacktop'

In the here-now is our Nemesis
And our destination Nowhere.

For the Record

Myth affirms where history must surmise,
If the dead could speak they'd tell us lies.

The Past

Done and fixed yet daily changing,
Look again — it's never quite the same.

A Country Road, A Tree
After 'Waiting for Godot'

We attend the neverending day
And waken to eternity renewed.

Amok Summery of Bloomsday

Bad choices, but Joyce's, beJasus!

Long away and far ago in the Cultic tweelight under the short rein of Headwood the Savant, a new day dawned — unique like any other — over the farcity of cuckolds and mudshells, universal quaquiversal, dublin up with myrth cerebrating a tumotley expoperiation of the roidisant in a collideoscope of vigours of speech, wordiplay and logorhythms.

a cryptic a crostic, a grinning fellow's joyshtick

Look upon these doubty wights, ye mighty, at this pair:

Stephen, deedless agonist, soulsmith in stognation, garrulsome and quarreloose, sighing for the sire who sailed away on shivery timbres with the muddlecrass of many layers, flailing himself under the fardels of a Hamnet complex to bear daneguilt for generations unborne.

Leopold, bereaved patriarch, pieceable and passedover, ruddiless athrift, ortcast from the lust drives of Wasrael (roll the readcall of whathaveyounames: O Donoghue, O Donovan, O Davis, O Dysseus) vragged to churchment, caught of conscience, tried of jewry, contemned to lief with whored liebe.

An indeterminate sentence — *eh, as you were, Erse.*

PURGATORIO: Devouring time ate of the clock

While the company of the round tower breaks fast in sacrificial slow time, uxorious Poldy is proffering burnt offering to Madame Pikehoses. These twain shall meet hereafter, shop-schlepping lionbold and outstriding stiff'un, eponym and epiphebe, strawling the corroded straits of the capitall's clutterways, clatterwheeze, glitterwares.

Plurabelle pause oftly till I end my song

Stephen, ineluctable pettygog selfpoortrade as a pulpable freud meant to diddle us, converses in alternating currents with the didactic D.C. (up to his old monkistricks) while golden lads go jabberwhacking hockeysticks, then tooks his pay into his pocket picking driftward at the agenbitten scarce of inwit.

Leopold, commercial travailler solicitous of pervertising, makes a forth in escorps to belay the late Pasde Deux in Glossinheaven interment camp nunc demeters, thence winds his weigh midst slackstrung lyres trading spaces in the dark titanic ells of massprint.

Unwholly communion

Smellsite quays of the kingdom, Leopold cast upon the waters, let them eat cake, fivehatted Eli — dodge the apostrophe, *howveyoubeenMrsBreen*, lifetimes landlord in aeternum loungerie undiesplay, thus to honour us and slaughterous the burden of loose draconian yappertites *roast and mashed here*, retreat to Davy Byrne's lucre whereof to dine on bread and wine *(with cheese and mustard)*.

Plurabelle phrase aptly till I end my song

In the babblic lieprayery (hush now!) Stephen holds forth on the geneallergy of the small town hero of the shickser bard of Thrucross-on-Celtwater, refracting on his own predicamenta, gossoon of goatsong. Enter stageyright: Metaphysician, whole thyself, divine the ills that ail thy soul and even more thy entelech. Are you choked with *Aridsdottle*?

Intermezzo: visceregal flauntulence

Postprandial proudcession perplosively premabulating *upupclippyclopupup* past present populous, public muniments and Poddle issewage.

Plurabelle praise wifely till I end my song

Poldypubscrawl in Goldworld with suites in many keys: K minor and Liddy Douce, Paltercock and Billy Doux wherewith fleurtation at barmaidsight feast — she snaps a mean garter for the slantstraw rat and here how he goes: jigjogjinglejaunty, the blue serge blazes in his clocksocked tanbooties a-triptoe true the twolips, part up, part open, squish, partunda! wafting strains of skewived Leonel, Don, Joe, Fanny and the nuntoo merry waif of Wexford who crossed both himself and that boyne whence no travailler...

Dissent into malestorm

At Bonny Carenone's hostillery talltelling stocks and sports, markets, courts, sportive kings and spurtive things: *Ayes, nays and bloompsadizzy.* Alas, tink, Otello tardy, cometh raging bull nonbefriending, be martyred or raise armed, green semite, domystic wanderful, blandishing smoulderpole in the faeces of Feignian phallusy.

Chants meeting at dusk

So pass they onthestranding, the littoral crepuscular merritime where Ophelia MacDowell, gamin and skittish, ailing from consumer praecox, swoons in the shallows under the rugged red glare of the darkening Bloom, who be mutejawlly misdebating with nary a word and wary a nod until — ohsuchsweetsorrow — anticline acts (sins of emission), wick undipped and lamp untrimmed.

INFERNO: Ten at pray in the Hippocratic temple

Mr Pureofaith, for all the madness in his methodism, must have been gaining indulgences in the sacrebleu of Extreme Conjunction, for here's the comesequence of their blissed ha-ha: Minnie brought to term again and and lying inlaid out for the birthing of her ninth surviving, whileaway the medicemen jestate shamantics over forty parse apprised in enceinte prostyle.

Walking down Mabbot Street, Here Comes Everybawdy

To while away worldpurgesnight at Cissy's menarecheery, licentioused premisses in wrathlicked distract, come studdents of lief, all prick and no penice, mightier than the sword, more porter than puta, sheiks all, shicks all, fond erinvolk. Enorgy of dissolutionment ensues inwith Leopold and Stephen entertwine their dreamwork of self excusation, transfixed by an orable zeitghast — a mummy, no lass — amidst blathera of boysterity and angrimoanious hicschanges until the crabbed boy defyles the light with cajole appraised, and a smashing time is had, by Chimminy (forthwitch Leopold makes rappareetion). Stephen stoned and Poldy pacemaker, straylamb and convasser, debouch into the nigh terre to be brought up short in a bruisy brush with a brace of British privates — O hideyoueyes sight!

PARADISO: Catechism beggaring the questor

Quasipaterfiliusque, prodtickle father and protocol son, having purrowled Montomenstreets and partwaken at curbsight brazierie with yearnspun glibtrotter Sal Peccaremale (nichtnamed Murphy), come throatstopped to the house of seven eccles — Behold, lordthiefinthenight hath rerentered! Sound the toxin, slag the fetid cough, loft alight the highburnian pastcall candle! Join in unisong eulogies of tallowmakers onsent Agnost's day!

Plurabelle pray swive me now I end my song

Soft! On furbelled beds of moly the former Marion Tweedy swoons in the deeps, ormered in panoply of reverie, tossing on the billows in the Oisin of Morpheus, feliciter in fideliter feasting on the freepast backoning to the herenow in eidertime. Maudlin Rose of Castellano seenyourarse moohairies, faultsome are Tilde, mad Oona, Daisy, Etty, Dolores, as under the moreish will she waits, she wants as ever was her wont to lie, to weep, purchase to dream, a consumption devouredly to be — whssst! — I hab taken you on a Moby's trip circontinuous, illbeit liffeylapping quadrature of the vicoish circle. Victoria's long rain is over and it's turned out fineagain — Endsleep!!

Ite, Missa Jest

Rem Tenui

Notes

p. 24: *The Locket*, a short story by Kate Chopin, composed in 1897, and first published in 1969.

p. 26: *Merrill's Marauders* (1962), written and directed by Samuel Fuller.

p. 28: *Les Parapluies de Cherbourg* (1964), written and directed by Jacques Demy.

p. 38: *Shoulder*, a play by Lorender Freeman.

p.38: *What is a Poem?*, a poem by Matt Hetherington.

p.39: *Two Lane Blacktop* (1971), written by Rudy Wurlitzer and directed by Monte Hellman.

p.39: *Waiting for Godot,* a play by Samuel Beckett.

John Tobin O'Fearna Flaus is Australian-born; Irish by extraction; Catholic by indoctrination; anarchist by conviction; and father of four.

From blue-collar beginnings in eastern Sydney, Flaus was a long-time associate of the Sydney Push. He worked as milk carter, plastic moulder (the old "78" records), and later as adult education organiser (the WEA of NSW). He has been a resident of Castlemaine, in Central Victoria, since the 1990's.

He has been writing and broadcasting film criticism intermittently since 1953. A part-time student at Sydney University from 1954 to 1971, he graduated with honours in English Literature under the supervision — and inspiration — of Bill Maidment.

Flaus went on to design and lecture in La Trobe University's inaugural Cinema Studies course from 1975. In 1977 he became a professional actor, and has since earned over 180 stage and screen credits. That career is now restricted by the onset of Alzheimer's disease.

Flaus wrote his first poem in 1996, at the age of 62. His first collection, *'Parallacts'*, featuring his original verse form, was published in 2012 by Mark Time Books.

www.ingramcontent.com/pod-product-compliance
Lightning Source LLC
Chambersburg PA
CBHW050448010526
44118CB00013B/1737